FAVORITE CLASSICS 1

arranged by DAVID CARR GLO

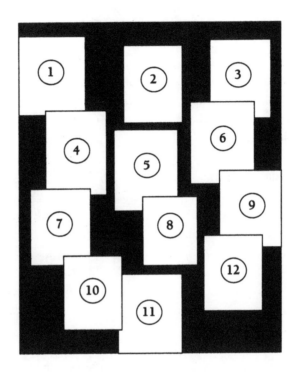

1. Johann Sebastian Bach
2. Ludwig van Beethoven
3. Johannes Brahms
4. Frederic Chopin
5. Edvard Grieg
6. George Frideric Handel
7. Franz Joseph Haydn
8. Felix Mendelssohn
9. Wolfgang Amadeus Mozart
10. Franz Schubert
11. Johann Strauss
12. Peter Ilyich Tchaikowsky

Editor: Carole Flatau
Cover Design & Art Layout: Debbie Johns Lipton

CONTENTS

Air

FRANZ JOSEPH HAYDN
Arranged by DAVID CARR GLOVER

EL9806

Artist's Life

JOHANN STRAUSS
Arranged by DAVID CARR GLOVER

Tempo di valse

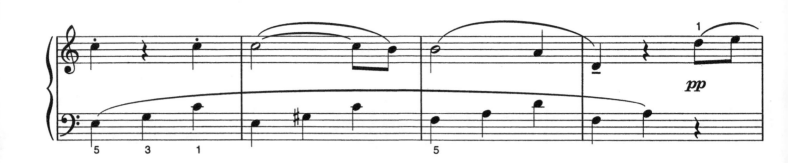

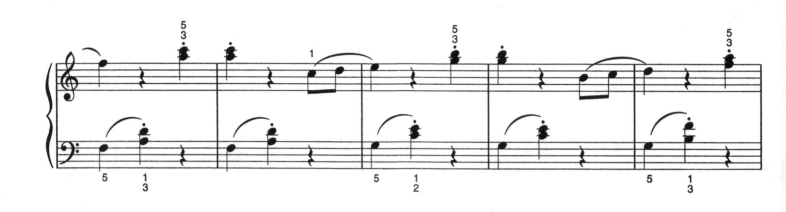

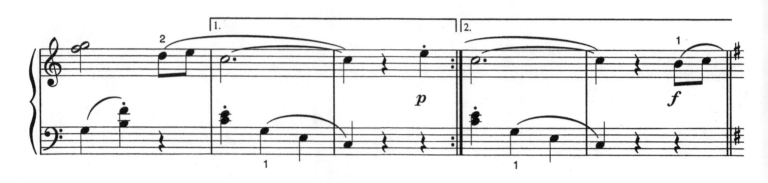

from "The Tales of Hoffman"

Barcarolle

JACQUES OFFENBACH
Arranged by DAVID CARR GLOVER

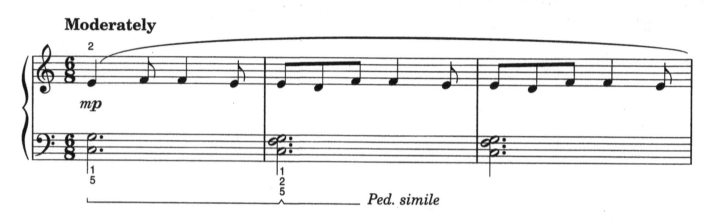

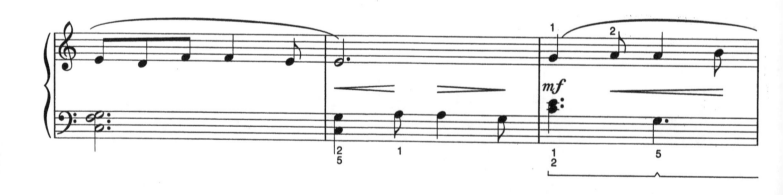

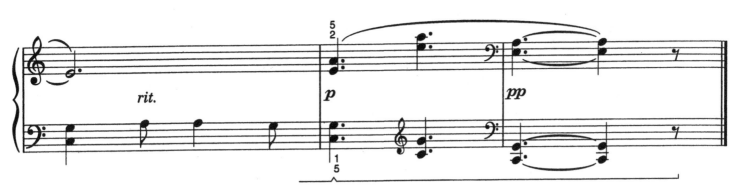

EL9806

from the Opera "Lohengrin"

Bridal Chorus

WAGNER
Arranged by DAVID CARR GLOVER

Majestically

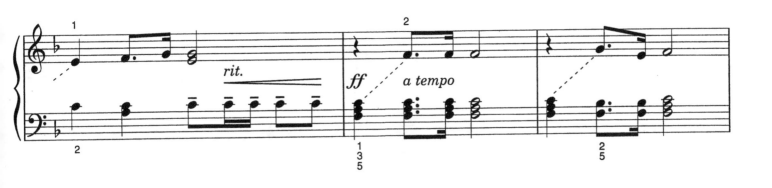

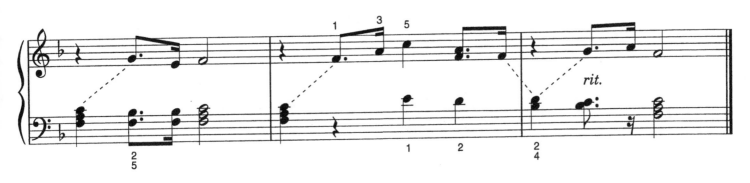

EL9806

from "Samson and Delilah"
Bacchanale

SAINT-SAËNS
Arranged by DAVID CARR GLOVER

Consolation
(Song Without Words)

FELIX MENDELSSOHN
Arranged by DAVID CARR GLOVER

Cradle Song

JOHANNES BRAHMS
Arranged by DAVID CARR GLOVER

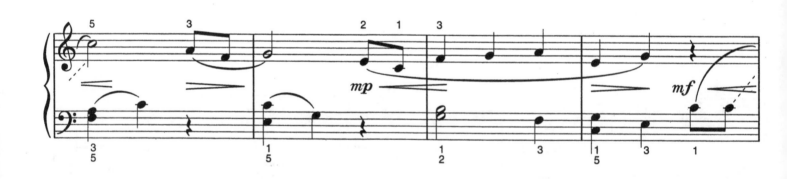

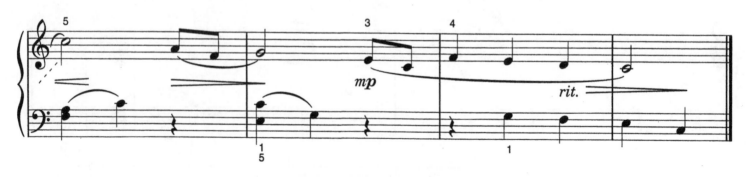

Cradle Song
(Wiegenlied)

FRANZ SCHUBERT
Arranged by DAVID CARR GLOVER

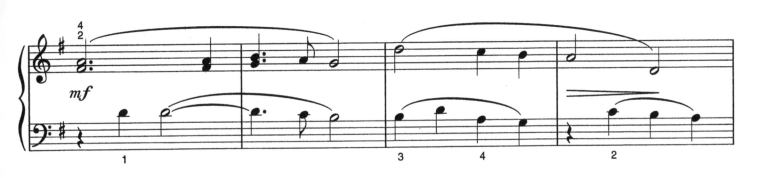

Elegie
Op. 10

JULES MASSENET
Arranged by DAVID CARR GLOVER

Slowly, with much feeling

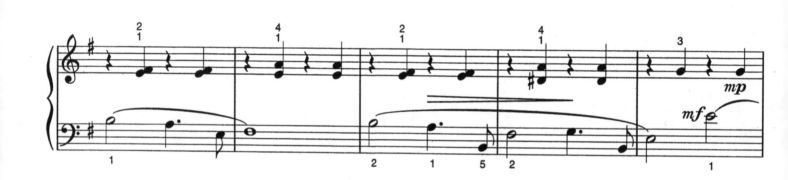

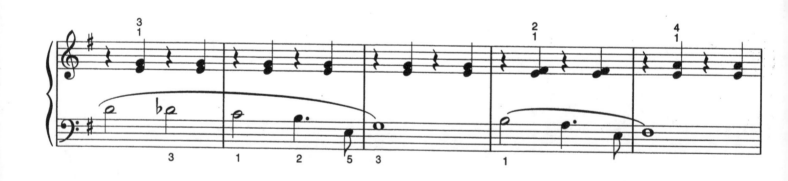

Etude
Op. 25, No. 9

FREDERIC CHOPIN
Arranged by DAVID CARR GLOVER

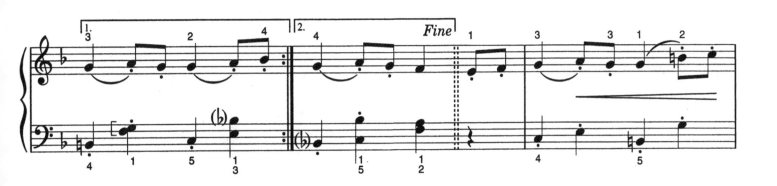

Etude

Op. 10, No. 3

FREDERIC CHOPIN
Arranged by DAVID CARR GLOVER

Lento ma non troppo

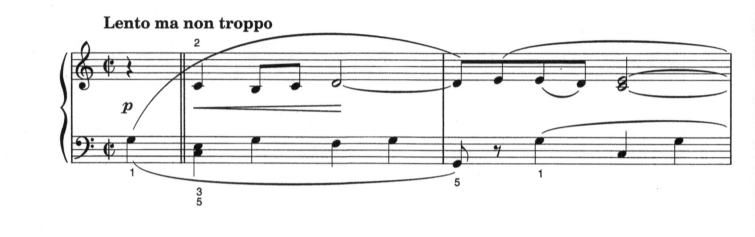

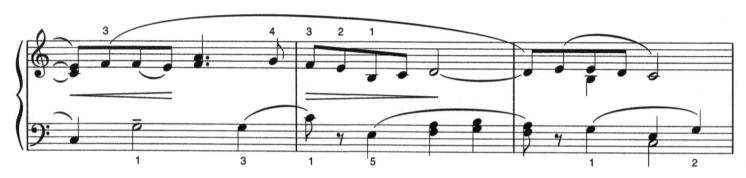

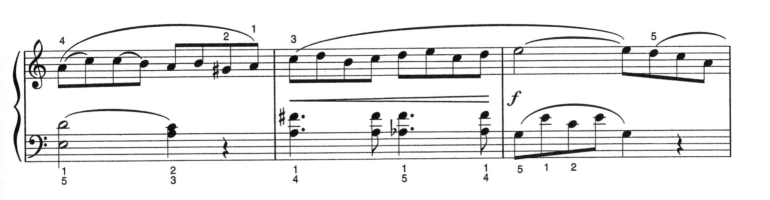

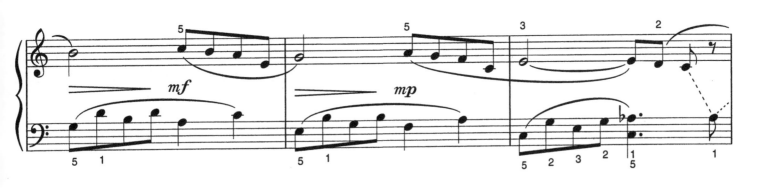

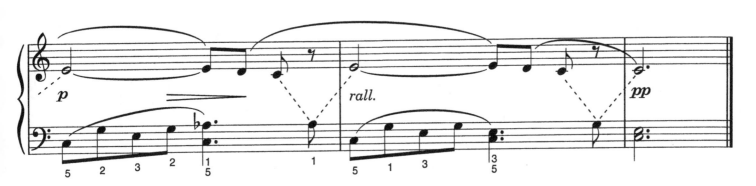

EL9806

The Emperor Waltz

JOHANN STRAUSS
Arranged by DAVID CARR GLOVER

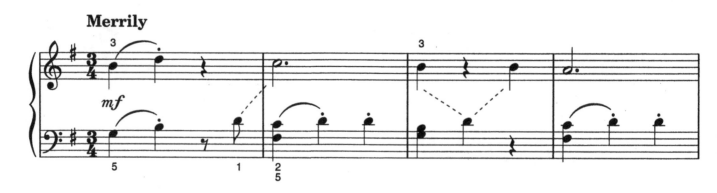

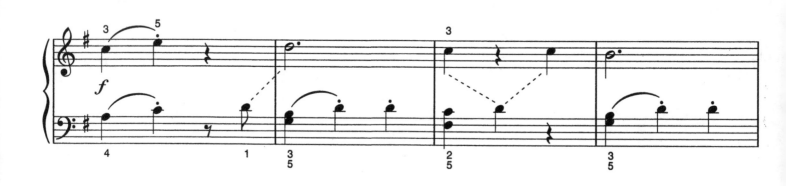

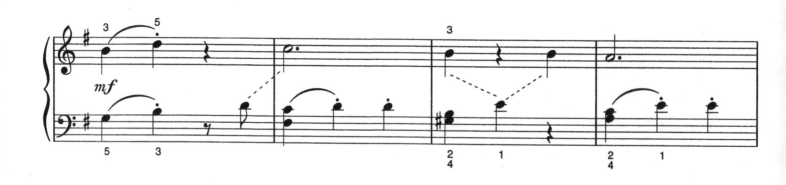

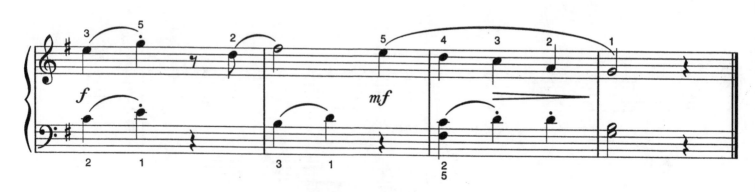

from Symphony No. 1

Finale

JOHANNES BRAHMS
Arranged by DAVID CARR GLOVER

Moderately fast

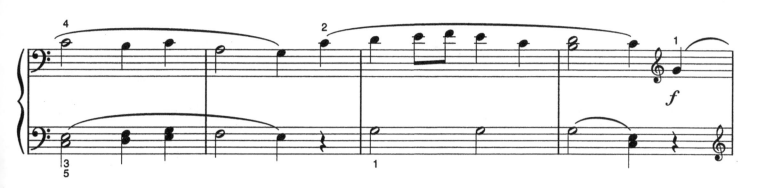

Fantasie Impromptu

FREDERIC CHOPIN
Arranged by DAVID CARR GLOVER

Moderate singing style

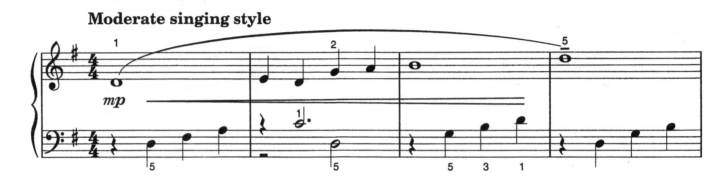

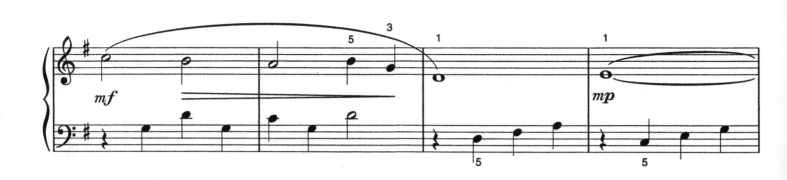

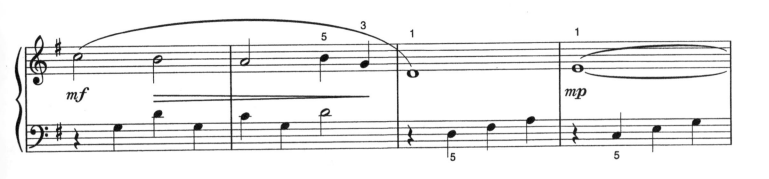

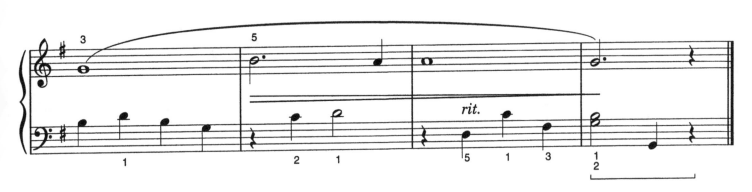

EL9806

from "Orpheus in the Underworld"

Gaité Parisienne

JACQUES OFFENBACH
Arranged by DAVID CARR GLOVER

from "Aida"

Grand March

GIUSEPPE VERDI
Arranged by DAVID CARR GLOVER

With dignity

Hungarian Dance No. 5

JOHANNES BRAHMS
Arranged by DAVID CARR GLOVER

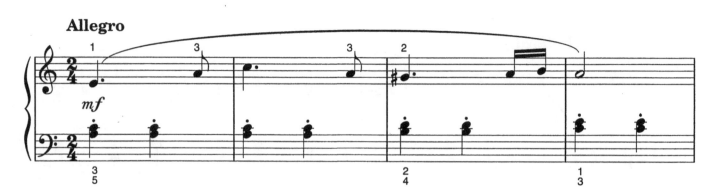

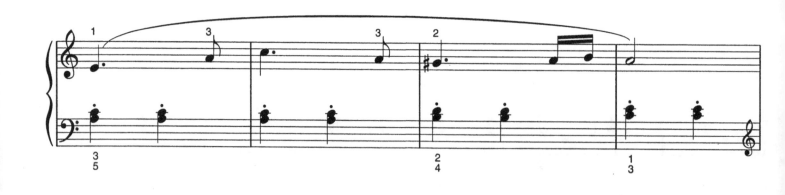

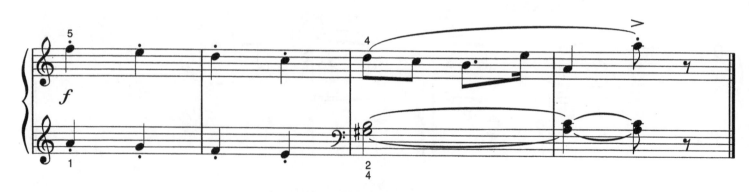

June

PETER ILYITCH TCHAIKOWSKY
Arranged by DAVID CARR GLOVER

In a singing style

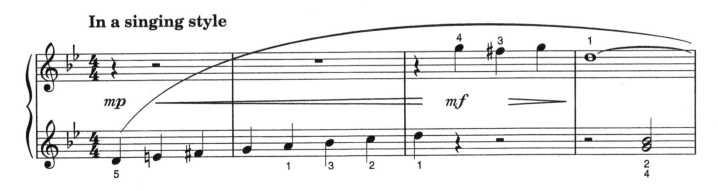

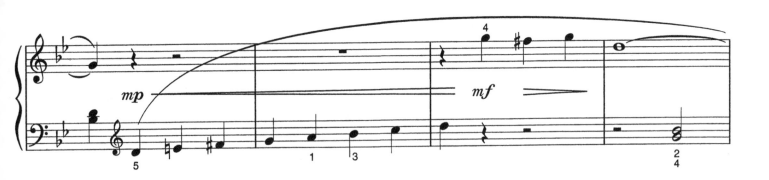

EL9806

from "Rigoletto"

La Donna é Mobile

GIUSEPPE VERDI
Arranged by DAVID CARR GLOVER

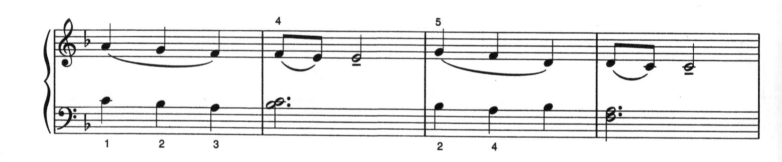

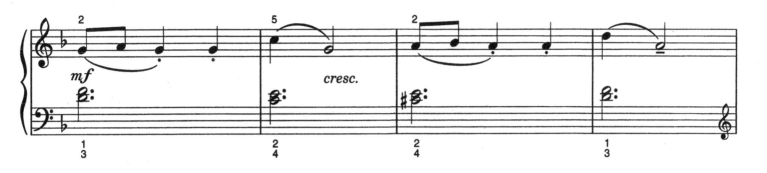

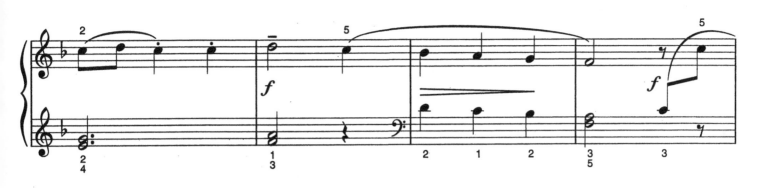

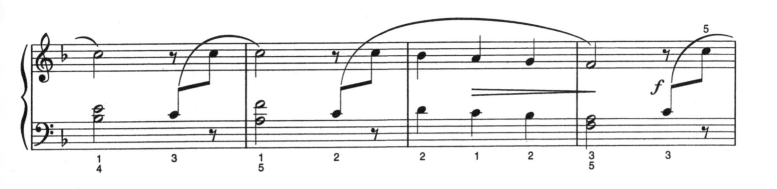

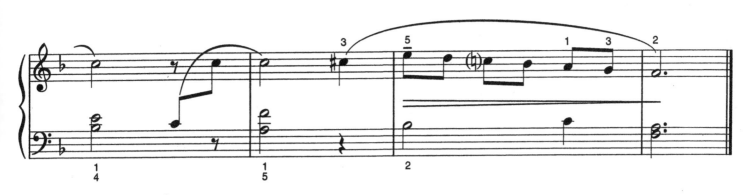

EL9806

from the Opera "Xerxes"

Largo

GEORGE FRIDERIC HANDEL
Arranged by DAVID CARR GLOVER

Slowly

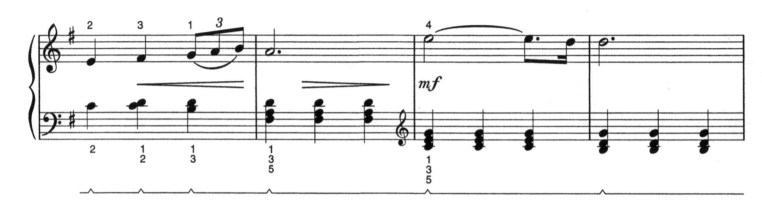

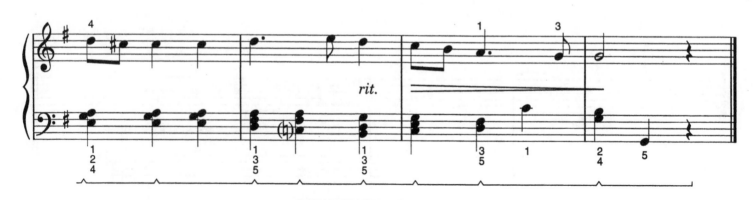

Liebestraume

FRANZ LISZT
Arranged by DAVID CARR GLOVER

March Militaire

FRANZ SCHUBERT
Arranged by DAVID CARR GLOVER

EL9806

Melody in F

ANTON RUBINSTEIN
Arranged by DAVID CARR GLOVER

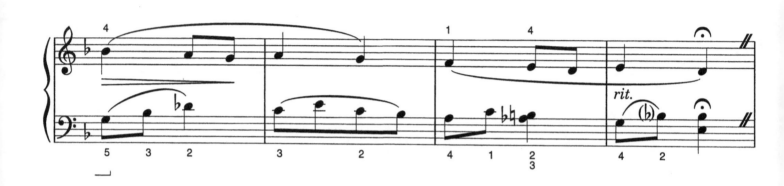

Piu mosso (a little faster)

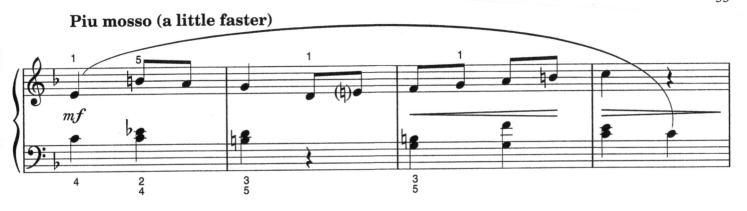

D.C. al Fine*

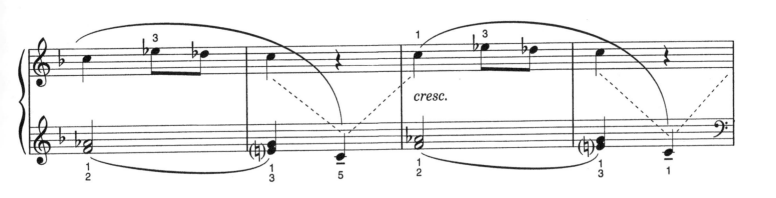

*Repeat from beginning to "Fine" (3rd ending only).

EL9806

Minuet

JOHANN SEBASTIAN BACH
Arranged by DAVID CARR GLOVER

Happily

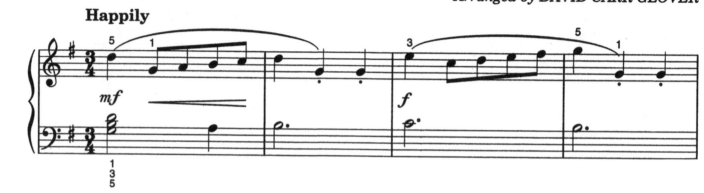

Musette

JOHANN SEBASTIAN BACH
Arranged by DAVID CARR GLOVER

Gaily

Minuet

LUDWIG VAN BEETHOVEN
Arranged by DAVID CARR GLOVER

EL9806

Minuet in G

LUDWIG VAN BEETHOVEN
Arranged by DAVID CARR GLOVER

Tempo di minuet

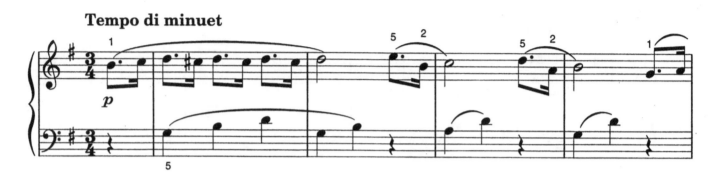

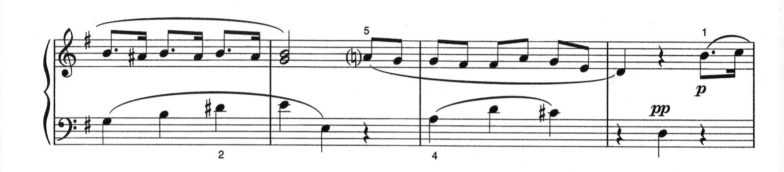

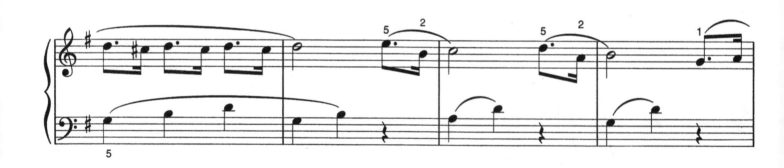

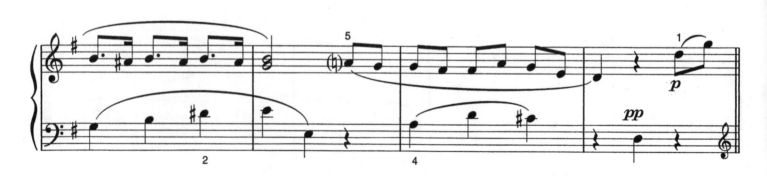

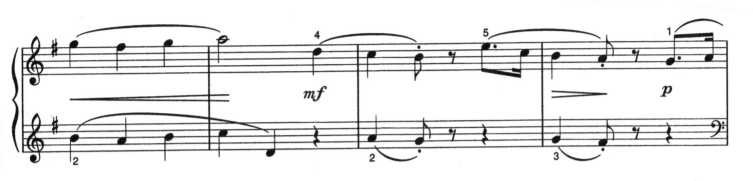

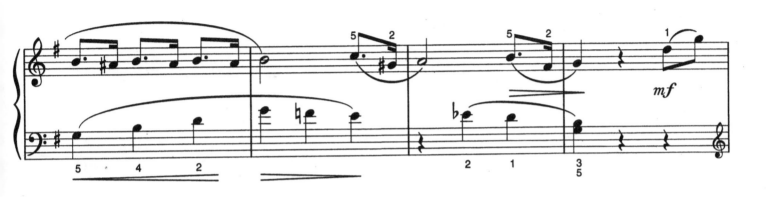

EL9806

Nocturne
Op. 9, No. 2

FREDERIC CHOPIN
Arranged by DAVID CARR GLOVER

Repeat from sign 𝄋 to Fine.

Norwegian Dance

EDVARD GRIEG
Arranged by DAVID CARR GLOVER

EL9806

Roses from the South

JOHANN STRAUSS
Arranged by DAVID CARR GLOVER

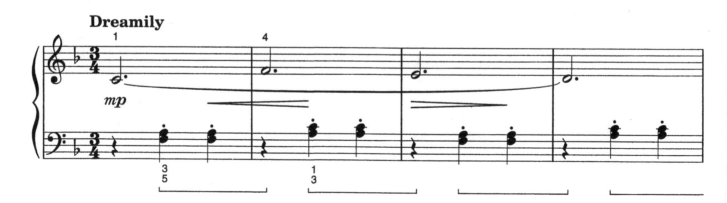

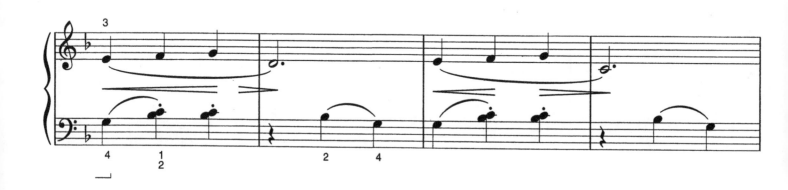

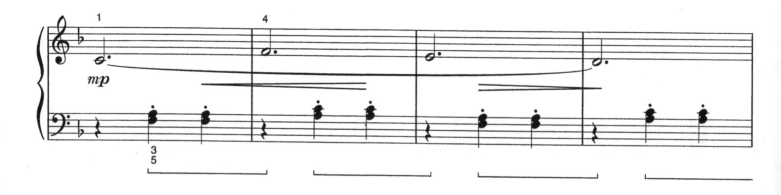

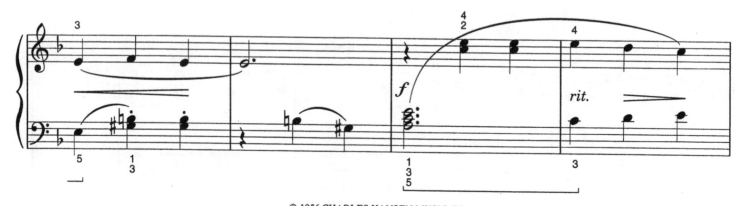

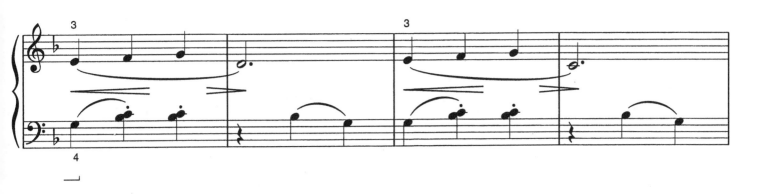

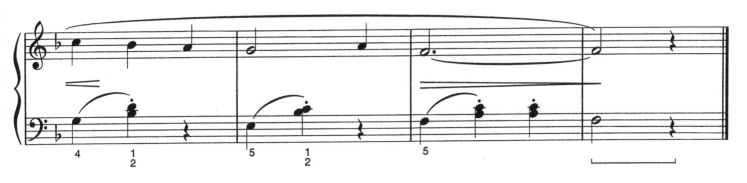

EL9806

Scheherazade

NICOLAI RIMSKY-KORSAKOV
Arranged by DAVID CARR GLOVER

Slowly, with much expression

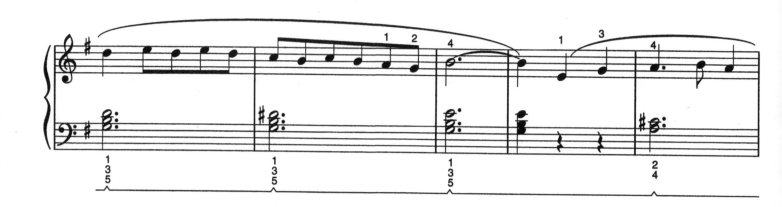

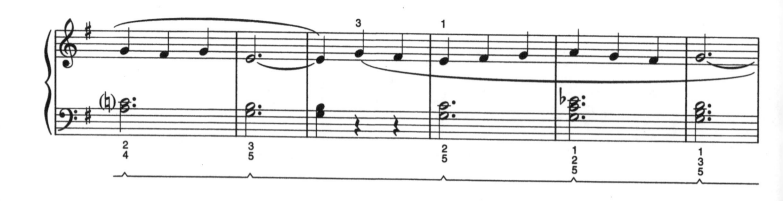

Prelude

FREDERIC CHOPIN
Arranged by DAVID CARR GLOVER

EL9806

Serenade

JOHANNES BRAHMS
Arranged by DAVID CARR GLOVER

from "The Sleeping Beauty"

Sleeping Beauty Waltz

PETER ILYITCH TCHAIKOWSKY
Arranged by DAVID CARR GLOVER

Flowing

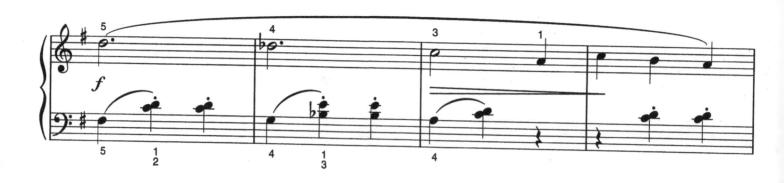

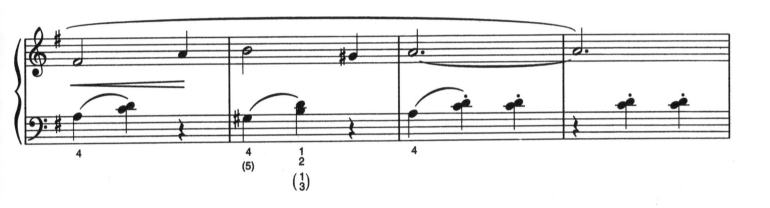

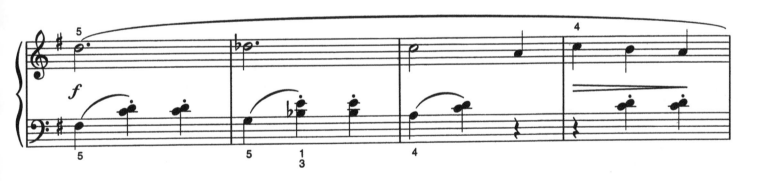

EL9806

from "Faust"

Soldiers Chorus

CHARLES GOUNOD
Arranged by DAVID CARR GLOVER

Moderately fast

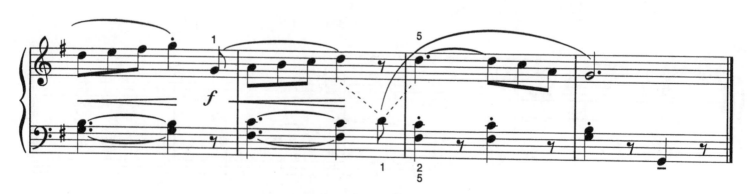

Spring Song

FELIX MENDELSSOHN
Arranged by DAVID CARR GLOVER

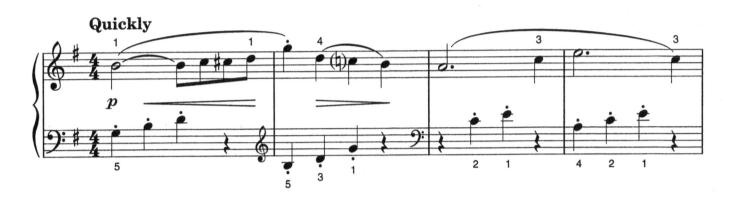

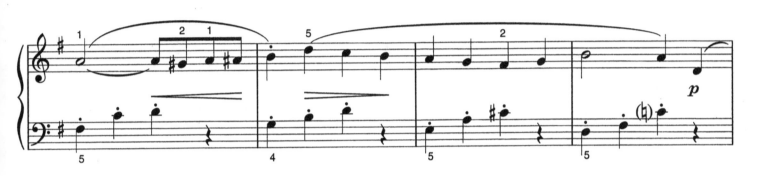

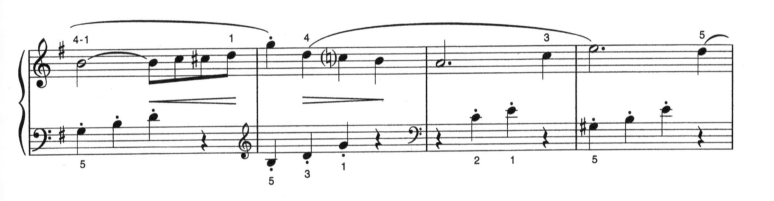

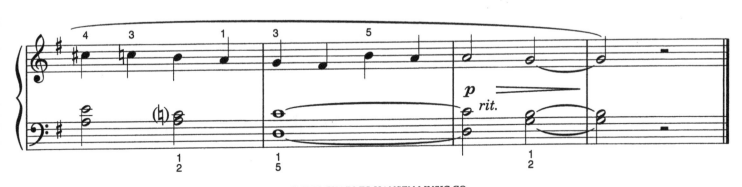

Tales from the Vienna Woods

JOHANN STRAUSS
Arranged by DAVID CARR GLOVER

Tempo di valse

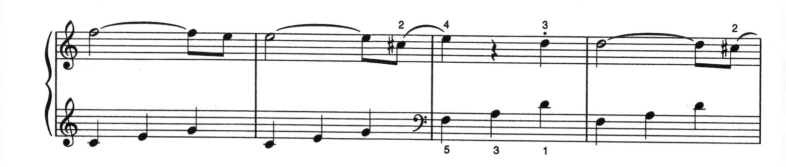

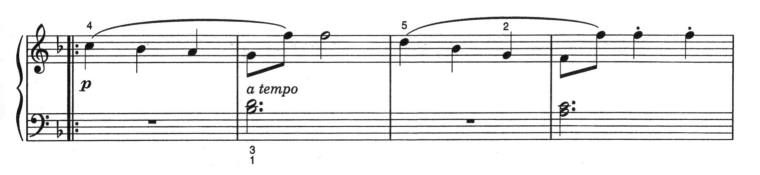

EL9806

Surprise Symphony

FRANZ JOSEPH HAYDN
Arranged by DAVID CARR GLOVER

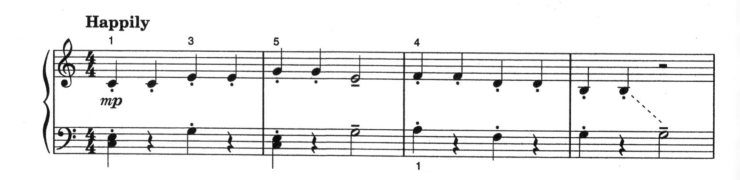

from "Carmen"

Toreador Song

GEORGES BIZET
Arranged by DAVID CARR GLOVER

EL9806

from "The Ruins of Athens"

Turkish March

LUDWIG VAN BEETHOVEN
Arranged by DAVID CARR GLOVER

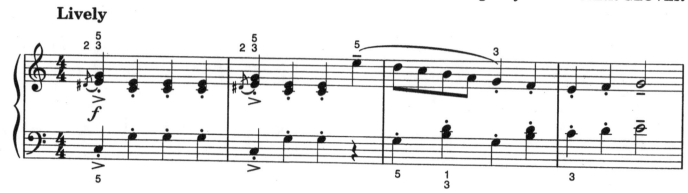

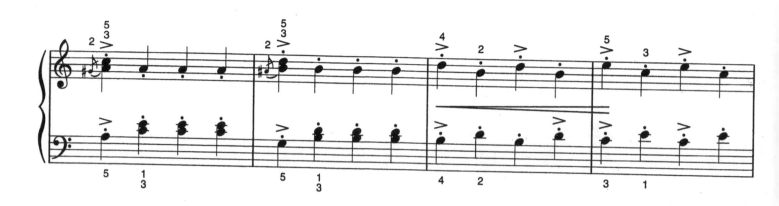

Unfinished Symphony

FRANZ SCHUBERT
Arranged by DAVID CARR GLOVER

Moving along, but not too fast

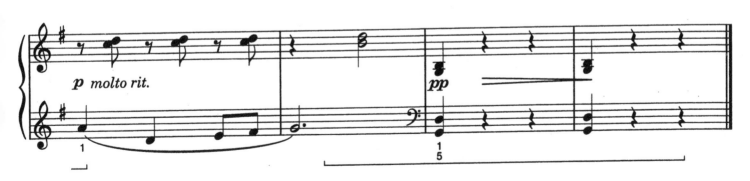

Vienna Life

JOHANN STRAUSS
Arranged by DAVID CARR GLOVER

Tempo di valse

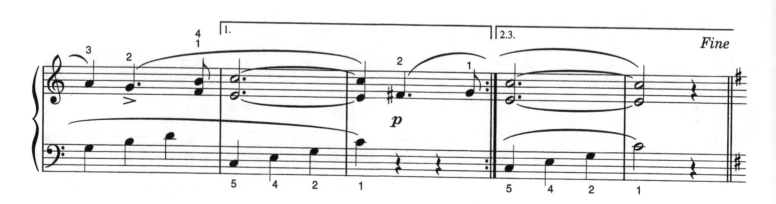

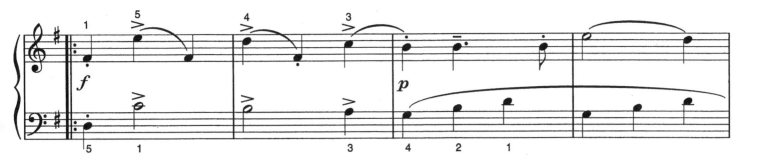

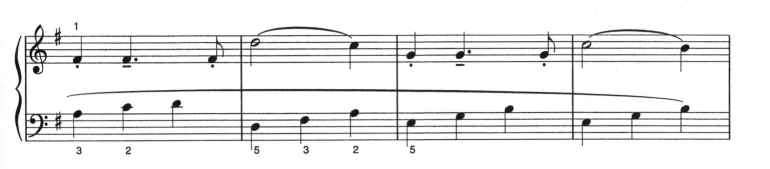

D.S. 𝄌 *al Fine*

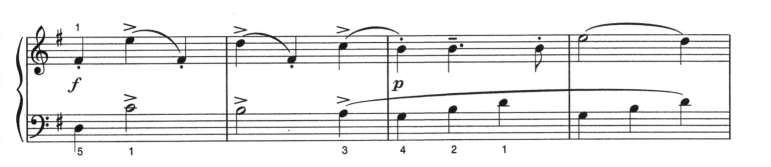

EL9806

Waltz

JOHANNES BRAHMS
Arranged by DAVID CARR GLOVER

Flowingly

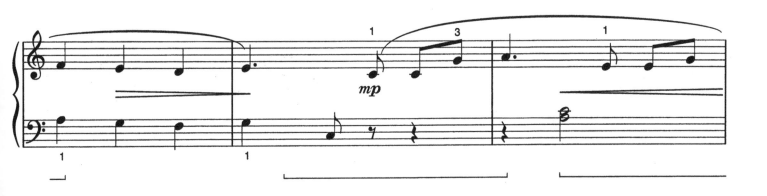

Waltz
Op. 18

FREDERIC CHOPIN
Arranged by DAVID CARR GLOVER

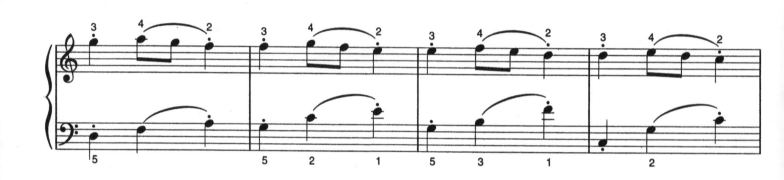

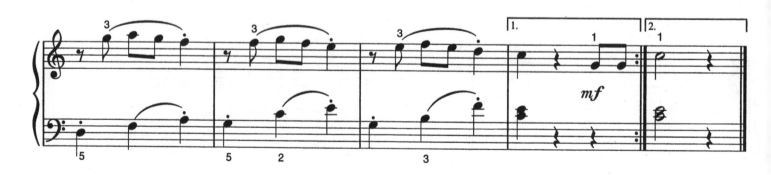

EL9806

Waltz

FRANZ SCHUBERT
Arranged by DAVID CARR GLOVER

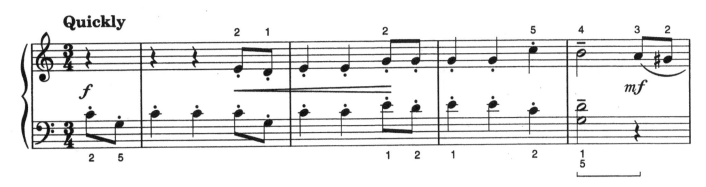

from "The Nutcracker"

Waltz of the Flowers

PETER ILYITCH TCHAIKOWSKY
Arranged by DAVID CARR GLOVER

Waltz in A Minor

Op. 34, No. 2

FREDERIC CHOPIN
Arranged by DAVID CARR GLOVER

In a singing style

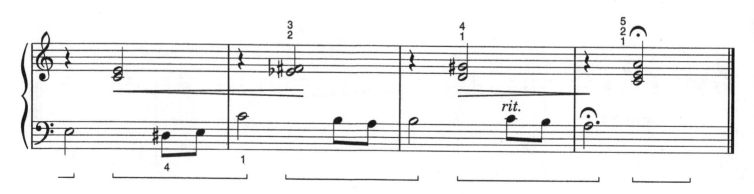

from "Sleeping Beauty"

Waltz of the Lilac Fairy

PETER ILYITCH TCHAIKOWSKY
Arranged by DAVID CARR GLOVER

Tempo di valse

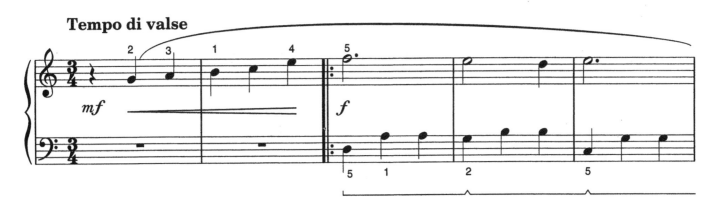

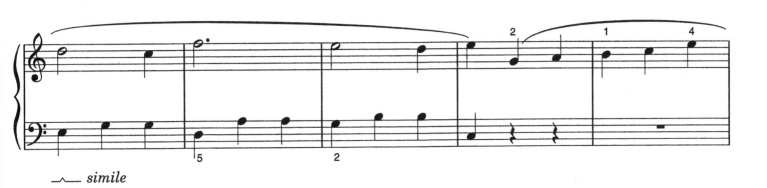

_⌣_ *simile*

EL9806

Waves of the Danube

IOSIF IVANOVICI
Arranged by DAVID CARR GLOVER

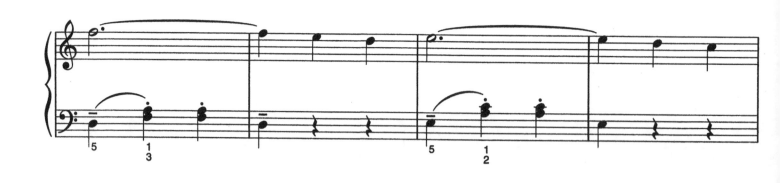

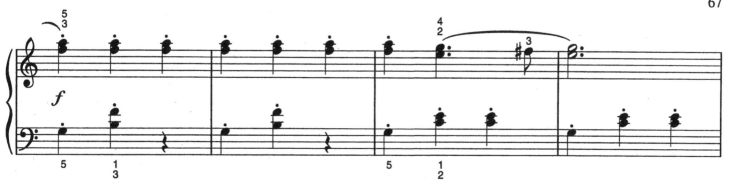

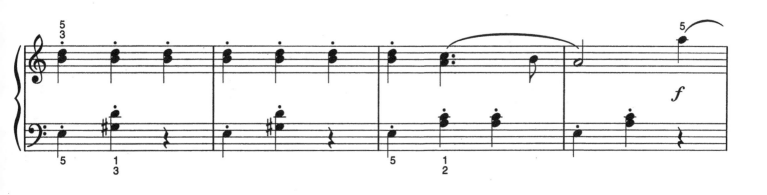

Wiegenlied
(Cradle Song)

WOLFGANG AMADEUS MOZART
Arranged by DAVID CARR GLOVER

Slowly, gently

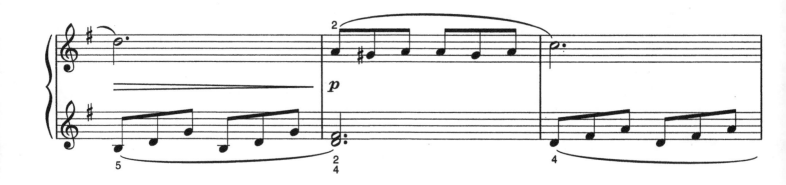

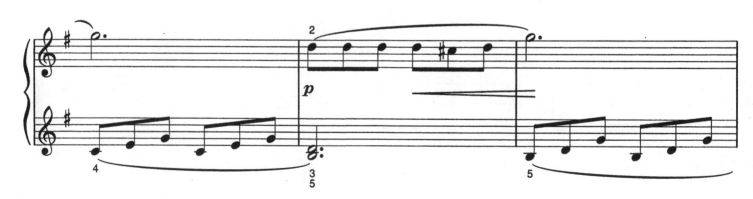

EL9806

Wine, Woman and Song

JOHANN STRAUSS
Arranged by DAVID CARR GLOVER

Tempo di valse

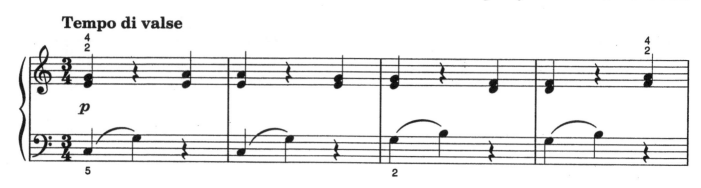

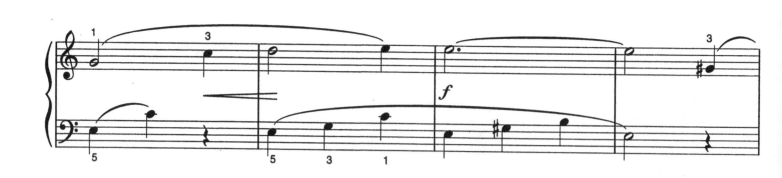

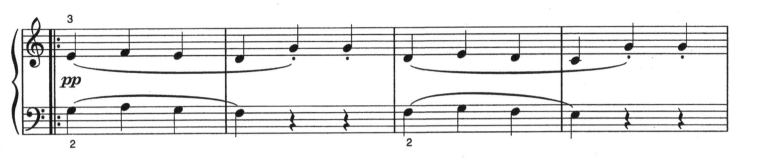

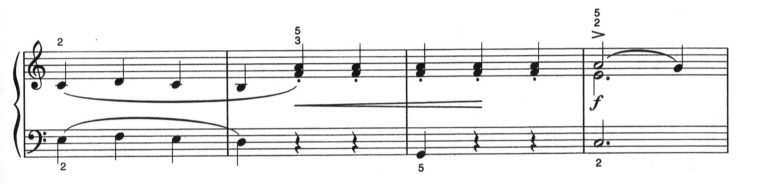

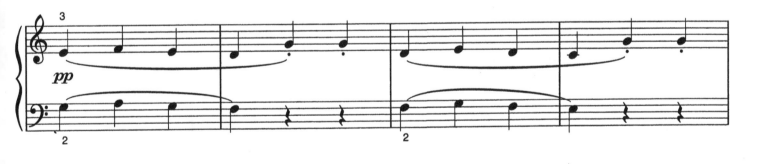

EL9806

from "Athalia"

War March of the Priests

FELIX MENDELSSOHN
Arranged by DAVID CARR GLOVER